What Does a
CONGRESSIONAL
REPRESENTATIVE Do?

David J. Jakubiak

PowerKiDS press.

New York

To David Esannason, soldier, friend, inspiration. Thank you.

Published in 2010 by The Rosen Publishing Group, Inc.
29 East 21st Street, New York, NY 10010

First Edition

Editor: Amelie von Zumbusch
Book Design: Julio Gil
Photo Researcher: Jessica Gerweck

Photo Credits: Cover, p. 14 Mandel Ngan/AFP/Getty Images; pp. 5, 9 Chip Somodevilla/Getty Images; pp. 6, 13, 17 Scott J. Ferrell/Congressional Quarterly/Getty Images; p. 10 Mark Wilson/ Getty Images; p. 14 Mandel Ngan/Getty Images; p. 18 Shutterstock.com; p. 21 Michael Tighe/ Hulton Archive/Getty Images.

Library of Congress Cataloging-in-Publication Data

Jakubiak, David J.
  What does a congressional representative do? / David J. Jakubiak.
    p. cm. — (How our government works)
  Includes index.
  ISBN 978-1-4358-9362-7 (library binding) — ISBN 978-1-4358-9820-2 (pbk.) —
ISBN 978-1-4358-9821-9 (6-pack)
  1. United States. Congress. House—Juvenile literature. 2. Legislators—United States—Juvenile literature. I. Title.
  JK1319.J35 2010
  328.73'072—dc22
                                                2009032390

Manufactured in the United States of America

CPSIA Compliance Information: Batch #WW10PK: For Further Information contact Rosen Publishing, New York, New York at 1-800-237-9932

CONTENTS

YOUR VOICE IN WASHINGTON

Every other year, the time comes to elect a congressional representative. The **candidates** for this important office can be seen on your television. Their names show up on signs along the road and on bumper stickers on cars. They promise to bring your voice to Washington, D.C.

A representative's job is to represent, or stand up for, the people in his or her community. Congressional representatives are members of the House of Representatives. The House is the larger of the two houses, or parts, of the U.S. Congress. Congress is the part of the **federal** government that makes laws.

Steny Hoyer (left) represents the people of southern Maryland in the House. Eric Cantor (right) was elected by the people of Virginia's Seventh Congressional District.

On January 6, 2009, members of the 111th House of Representatives were sworn in. They promised to follow the U.S. Constitution.

A VERY FULL HOUSE

There are 435 members of the House of Representatives. Each representative is elected by voters from a **congressional district** within a state.

A state's **population** sets the number of representatives that state sends to the House. States where more people live have more districts. These states send more representatives. For example, California is the state with the highest population. It has a representative from each of its 53 districts. However, Alaska, Delaware, Montana, North Dakota, South Dakota, Vermont, and Wyoming each have just one representative.

Congress has not added members to the House since 1911. In recent years, it has considered adding two more seats. They would likely go to Utah and Washington, D.C.

CHOOSING A REPRESENTATIVE

Elections for the House are held in November. People watch election results closely. They want to know who won in their district and which **political** party won the most seats overall. Today, the United States has two main political parties, the Democrats and Republicans.

Every 10 years, the government holds a census to count people. The count sets how many representatives each state is allowed. State governments then lay out their districts.

In 1994, the Republican Party had not held a majority of House seats for 40 years. Then, Georgia representative Newt Gingrich helped create the Contract with America. This plan promised that Republicans would cut spending. In the next few elections, Republicans won a majority in the House.

In 2006, Patrick Murphy (center) ran for representative from Pennsylvania's Eighth Congressional District. He won and began serving in January 2007.

In 2007, Steny Hoyer (left) was voted house majority leader, while Jim Clyburn (right) was elected majority whip. Whips count and try to "whip up" votes.

THE HOUSE'S LEADERSHIP

On January 4, 2007, California representative Nancy Pelosi was elected the first woman Speaker of the House. She called for Congress to make "a new America that is strong, secure, and a respected leader among the community of nations."

At the start of each Congress, representatives elect a Speaker to lead the House. This is a powerful job since the Speaker can pick members to speak on the House floor. The Speaker can also send bills to House **committees**. Other House leaders include the majority leader, who works with the Speaker, and the minority leader, who leads the party with fewer members.

BILLS THAT MAKE A DIFFERENCE

The job of congressional representatives is to make sure the bills they pass are good for the people they serve. All bills having to do with taxes must start in the House. In recent years, the House has also passed bills to help the **environment** and spend money on job creation.

In 1972, Representative Patsy Mink, of Hawaii, wrote a bill to give women and girls the same chances boys and men have in schools. The bill, known as Title IX, passed. It especially helped girls and women get chances to play sports. At the time the bill passed, only 300,000 girls were playing high-school sports. Today, more than 3 million are.

Here, Representative David Obey (left) and Representative Ray LaHood (right) talk about a 2007 bill to spend more money on the war in Iraq.

In 2009, President Barack Obama (center) signed a bill to help keep children from smoking. Representatives who had worked on the bill watched him sign it.

WORKING WITH THE SENATE

After the House votes to pass a bill, that bill still must pass the **Senate**. In the same way, bills that start in the Senate must be passed by the House. Both the House and the Senate can make changes to bills. Sometimes, the two houses pass bills that are close but do not match. Then, representatives and senators get together in a conference committee to work out the differences between the two bills.

> If the president turns down, or vetoes, a bill, it can go back to Congress. If two-thirds of the House and Senate vote for it again, it will become a law.

Once both houses of Congress have passed a bill, it goes to the president. If the president signs it, the bill becomes a law.

THE HOUSE INQUIRES

Congressional representatives work in groups called committees. The House has 20 standing committees. These ongoing committees cover subjects such as education, the military, and farming.

One job of committees is to work on bills. Committees also inquire into important matters. One example of this power came in 1974. The House Judiciary Committee held hearings to impeach President Richard Nixon. Impeaching is charging a government official with breaking the law. The House is the only body that can impeach a president. On July 27, 1974, the committee charged Nixon in an article of impeachment. On August 8, Nixon stepped down.

Every House committee has a chair, or head. In 2009, John Conyers, the chair of the House Judiciary Committee, led hearings on how prisoners are treated.

People who want to learn about the House of Representatives can visit the Capitol. There are tours of the building almost every day of the year.

AT HOME IN THEIR OWN CHAMBER

The House of Representatives meets in a chamber, or room, on the second floor of the South Wing of the Capitol. Construction on the Capitol began in 1793. The building was considered complete in 1826. By 1850, though, the country had grown and the building needed to be made bigger. In 1857, the House of Representatives moved into the chamber it still uses today.

The House chamber includes 448 seats facing the rostrum. The rostrum looks like a large raised desk. It is where the Speaker of the House sits.

The Cannon House Office Building, Longworth House Office Building, and Rayburn House Office Building all have extra space for representatives and committee meetings.

SHAPING AMERICA

In January 1918, the House talked about giving women the right to vote. The only woman representative, Jeannette Rankin, of Montana, opened the talk. "How shall we answer the **challenge**, gentlemen?" she asked. Two years later, women finally got the vote.

Representatives shape the nation. In 1865, Representative James Mitchell Ashley, of Ohio, helped end **slavery** with the **Thirteenth Amendment**. New York representative Shirley Chisholm, who served from 1969 to 1983, worked for equality for all people. Representative Tip O'Neill was the Speaker from 1977 to 1986. He never forgot the people of Boston, Massachusetts, who had elected him. "All politics is local," he would say.

Shirley Chisholm, seen here, worked to make schools better for all children. She also tried to find ways to help poor children and their families.

TODAY'S HOUSE OF REPRESENTATIVES

Many of the biggest questions facing our country today are being worked on in the House of Representatives. Representatives such as George Miller, of California, and Judy Biggert, of Illinois, have taken steps to improve schools. Representatives Solomon Ortiz, of Texas, and J. Randy Forbes, of Virginia, worked to keep the nation safe.

Representatives need to hear from the people they serve. Hearing from their **constituents** helps them figure out what problems need fixing. Do you know the name of your representative? You can find out on the House of Representatives Web site. You can also discover what your representative is doing in Washington, D.C.

GLOSSARY

candidates (KAN-dih-dayts) People who run in an election.

challenge (CHA-lenj) Something that requires extra effort.

committees (kuh-MIH-teez) Groups of people directed to oversee or consider a matter.

congressional district (kun-GRESH-nul DIS-trikt) The area where people who vote for one member of the House of Representatives live.

constituents (kun-STICH-wents) People who elect others to a public office.

environment (en-VY-ern-ment) All the living things and conditions of a place.

federal (FEH-duh-rul) Having to do with the work of government or public affairs.

political (puh-LIH-tih-kul) Having to do with governments and elections.

population (pop-yoo-LAY-shun) The number of people living in an area.

Senate (SEH-nit) A law-making part of the U.S. government.

slavery (SLAY-vuh-ree) The system of one person "owning" another.

Thirteenth Amendment (thur-TEENTH uh-MEND-ment) The article added to the U.S. Constitution that outlawed slavery.

INDEX

WEB SITES

Due to the changing nature of Internet links, PowerKids Press has developed an online list of Web sites related to the subject of this book. This site is updated regularly. Please use this link to access the list:
www.powerkidslinks.com/hogw/congress/